D1365114

Animal Trainer

Trudi Strain Trueit

Cavendish
Square

New York

Published in 2014 by Cavendish Square Publishing, LLC
303 Park Avenue South, Suite 1247, New York, NY 10010

Library of Congress Cataloging-in-Publication Data
Trueit, Trudi Strain.
Animal trainer / by Trudi Strain Trueit.
p. cm. — (Careers with animals)
Includes index.
ISBN 978-1-62712-461-4 (hardcover) ISBN 978-1-62712-462-1 (paperback) ISBN 978-1-62712-463-8 (ebook)
1. Animal trainers — Juvenile literature. 2. Animal training — Vocational guidance — Juvenile literature. I. Trueit, Trudi Strain. II. Title.
GV1829.T74 2014
636.08—dc23

J636.08
TRU
(2014)

Editorial Director: Dean Miller
Senior Editor: Peter Mavrikis
Copy Editor: Cynthia Roby
Art Director: Jeffrey Talbot
Designer: Amy Greenan
Photo Researcher: Julie Alissi, J8 Media
Production Manager: Jennifer Ryder-Talbot
Production Editor: Andrew Coddington

The photographs in this book are used by permission and through the courtesy of: Cover photo by © Juniors Bildarchiv GmbH/Alamy. AP Photo/Ted S. Warren, 4; Patrick Pleul/dpa/picturealliance/Newscom, 6; Baltimore Sun/Contributor/McClatchyTribune/Getty Images, 7; © Zick, Jochen/Keystone Pressedienst/ZUMA Press, 9; St Petersburg Times/ZUMAPRESS/Newscom, 9; Siegfried Kuttig/imag / imagebroker.net / SuperStock, 11; Taylor S. Kennedy/National Geographic/Getty Images, 12; © AP Images, 14; imagebroker.net / SuperStock, 15; Nordic Photos/ SuperStock, 16; ©McPHOTO, 18; gorillaimages/Shutterstock.com, 20; Annie Griffiths Belt/National Geographic/Getty Images, 21; David Silverman/Staff/Getty Images News/Getty Images, 21; © Renee Jones Schneider/Minneapolis Star Tribune/ZUMAPRESS.com, 23; Thinkstock/Comstock Images/Getty Images, 24; Boston Globe/Contributor/Boston Globe/Getty Images, 26; © AP Images, 27; Tom Bear/Aurora/Getty Images, 28; James Tourtellotte, U.S. Customs and Border Protection/CBP Airport/http://www.cbp.gov/xp/cgov/newsroom/photo_gallery/afc/cbp_protecting_america/08_airportbeag.xml, 29; Photographer's Mate 1st Class Arlo K. Abrahamson/ US Navy 030302-N-5362A-009 Military working dog, Camp Patriot, Kuwait.jpg/United States Navy, 30; Andrea Booher/ FEMA - 40689 - Valley Water Rescue member, Mike Knorr and search dog, ^quot,Barnaby^quot, in North Dakota.jpg/FEMA Photo Library, 31; Paul J. Richards/Staff/AFP/Getty Images, 33; Inti St. Clair/Photographer's Choice RF/Getty Images, 34; Mikhail Pogosov/Shutterstock.com, 36; AFP/Staff/AFP/Getty Images, 37; Cusp / SuperStock, 39; AFP/Stringer/AFP/Getty Images, 40; Andy Richter/Aurora+/Getty Images, 43; Altrendo/altrendo travel/Getty Images, 44; The Washington Post/Contributor/The Washington Post/Getty Images, 46; © AP Photo/Jessica Hill, 47; CORDIER Sylvain/hemis.fr/Getty Images, 48; Stuart Westmorland/The Image Bank/Getty Images, 51; © Keystone Pressedienst/ZUMAPRESS.com, 52; © H Schmidt-Roeger, 54; © AP Photo/Elise Amendola, 56; Jake Curtis/Rise/Getty Images, 57.

Printed in the United States of America

CONTENTS

ONE

Teacher's Pets

I t's the first day of school. A few students squirm but everyone in the room seems to be on their best behavior. "The first class is usually pretty chaotic," says Jeanette Fix, surveying her crop of new students. "But you're all so quiet." She isn't referring to the people. She is talking to the dogs.

Jeanette is a **canine** trainer and behaviorist. For an hour each week over the next two months, she will take eight dogs and their owners through a basic obedience course. The dogs will learn commands, such as "stay," "sit," and "leave it." Their owners will learn much more. As they begin to view the world through a dog's eyes, they will see the importance of being the leader in their family "pack." They will realize the mistakes they make that unintentionally reinforce bad habits. Most of all, they will discover ways to interact with their pets to help build a strong, lasting bond.

"It's exciting to see the transformations," says Jeanette, an instructor with Canine Behavior Center of Seattle. "So many people come here with no idea of how to even communicate with their dog. But by graduation, they are confident and comfortable. They understand how their dog thinks and how their relationship works."

Although she's had pets since childhood, Jeanette didn't set out to be a dog trainer. "I always knew I wanted to do something with animals," she recalls, "but

(Opposite) Many pet owners enroll in classes to learn how to train their animals. Sisco, Scrat, and Dodger (left to right) take obedience classes from their owner, Sarah Casey, in their DuPont, WA, home.

Many future dog trainers practice with their pets. Stefanie Wilke hones her skills by providing her dogs Maggie, Lena, and Peanut (L-R) professional lessons in good behavior.

I didn't know what was out there. I didn't yet have my direction." Like Jeanette, most professional animal trainers love animals. Many began by training their own birds, dogs, cats, or horses when they were young. They may have volunteered at a local shelter, veterinary clinic, or dog training school. After high school, they took one of many paths to enter the profession. Some earned one or more college degrees. Others attended a private training school. And still others learned on the job. That's how Jeanette started. By coincidence, she answered an advertisement for office help at what turned out to be Canine Behavior Center. She was hired and when a training position became available, Jeanette didn't let the opportunity pass. She read books, watched videos, and **apprenticed** with another trainer until she was ready to instruct her first class. That was 22 years ago.

Now, Jeanette leads two to three obedience classes per night, three evenings a week. She also teaches **dog agility** courses. During the day, she sees clients in their homes for private training sessions or to help resolve behavioral problems, such as aggression, anxiety, or housebreaking. Jeanette still works in the front office, too. "My life is busy," she laughs. "But it would get pretty boring if there were no challenges, right?"

A Kind Hand

In the past, animal training might have involved the use of force or punishment that hurt the animal mentally or physically. Modern training techniques emphasize respect, compassion, and safety for the animal. Even so, some trainers still use harsh methods. This is why it's important for anyone considering this career to thoroughly research educational routes before committing to one. None of the animal trainers profiled in this book use or condone abusive training methods.

Assistance dogs are trained to work calmly and quietly on harness, leash, or other tether. They are also specifically trained to perform three or more tasks to make their owners' disability less severe.

Bridging the Gap

According to the Department of Labor, there are more than 46,000 animal trainers in the United States. They work in various settings, from animal shelters to racetracks to military bases. Trainers may prepare animals for such things as adoption into new homes, education, sports and competition, law enforcement, homeland security, military service, and to aid people with disabilities.

Most animal trainers instruct companion animals (dogs and cats) or **equines** (horses). Some work with wildlife, such as zoo or marine animals. Trainers teach animals to perform certain skills or behaviors, either on command or on their own. Their work may yield remarkable results. To a child in a wheelchair, riding a trained horse can mean freedom. To a

Talk to the Animals... and People!

Most trainers have a way with animals, but would it surprise you to learn an animal trainer needs to connect with people, too? Dog and horse trainers must have good verbal skills to teach owners how to communicate with their animals. Wildlife and marine mammal trainers often conduct public presentations and interactive programs. In addition to being a people person, a trainer must also be:

- a patient and respectful teacher
- not afraid to get dirty, sweaty, wet, or cold!
- strong and physically fit
- willing to work long hours, including nights, weekends, and holidays
- prepared to work a second job, because animal training is, traditionally, a lower paying field
- skilled in business and marketing (many trainers are self-employed)

soldier in a war zone, a trained military dog can be a lifesaver. To anyone who is lonely, a trained pet can be a loyal friend.

Back at day one of dog obedience school, Jeanette is teaching the command "let's go," meaning it's time to walk. She tells everyone to clearly say their dog's name and the command, and then give a gentle tug on the leash, turn, and step off. She borrows Jack, a golden retriever, from his owner to demonstrate. When Jack does something wrong, Jeanette starts again. But the instant he gets it right, his teacher cries, "Good boy!" Soon, Jack figures out that walking on command will earn him the praise he wants. Now it's time for the rest of the class to try. The large floor is, suddenly, teeming with dogs and people, zigzagging in different directions. The trainer moves among them with ease, repeating instructions and guiding those who are having trouble. "Talk to your dogs," Jeanette calls. "Have fun. You are here for a relationship!"

It is natural for a puppy to want to follow a pack leader. For these golden retriever puppies to grow into healthy, balanced adult dogs, disciplinary training must begin from day one.

TWO

Training the Trainers

hat animals would you like to train? Dogs? Dolphins? Or maybe you aren't yet sure. The educational path you'll take depends on the animal(s) you decide to work with. Animal trainers in the United States do not need to meet any specific educational requirements. Even so, many employers have established their own hiring standards that you'll want to research. Also, there are recommended paths of study for the major areas of the field that may help improve your chances of getting hired. Animal training is a popular profession. More people want to be trainers than there are jobs available. Getting a good education is key in helping you gain a competitive edge.

Adventures with Animals

An animal trainer needs to understand how different species behave and function—that includes humans. Middle and high school students wanting to pursue the profession should take classes in psychology, biology, and anatomy. Much of a trainer's duties involve dealing with people, so a curriculum should also include language arts classes, such as creative writing, journalism, speech, and drama. Because many trainers are self-employed, students should take courses that prepare them to manage their own businesses. These

(Opposite) Some animal trainers choose to work with large and potentially dangerous animals such as lions, tigers, and elephants. The length of training can last anywhere from a few days to several months depending on the behavior that the trainer is tasked to reinforce.

Trixtan, a Blue Merle Collie, receives private at-home training sessions provided by Amy Robinson. Trixtan's owner, Myles Blane, is learning to give instructions.

include math, accounting, computer software applications, web design, marketing, advertising, and public relations. Academic counselors recommend maintaining a B average, or a grade point average (GPA) of 3.0 or above. Good grades will be an advantage when applying to college. Students should also join school clubs that focus on science, business, and leadership.

For an animal trainer, nothing beats experience! Do you have a dog? Take your canine friend through an obedience class. The American Kennel Club (AKC) offers courses through many of its local clubs. AKC also sponsors the Canine Good Citizen Program, a short, introductory dog ownership class that may lead to additional training in obedience, agility, tracking, or performance events. Some **service dog** trainers, such as Assistance Dogs of the West in Santa Fe, New Mexico, offer classes that teach students how to train service dogs. Look for a similar program in your area. You can also volunteer to work for a private dog trainer, groomer, dog walker, pet sitter, animal shelter, veterinarian, or wildlife sanctuary. To gain experience with horses, work at a barn under the supervision of a horse trainer. Learn to do everything from grooming to cleaning stalls. Professional horse trainers must also be outstanding riders, so take riding lessons. If possible, participate in shows

Get Your Feet Wet

Many of the marine mammal parks and centers in North America provide students the chance to work alongside a professional trainer to see what the job entails. Students may assist a trainer in feeding, instructing, exercising, and playing with the dolphins, sea otters, and other marine animals. Fees range from a few hundred dollars to be a "trainer for a day" to $1,500 or more for a week of resident summer camp. Visit the International Marine Animal Trainers' Association (IMATA) website for a list of facilities that offer hands-on programs for young people.

Horse trainers often use training aids for the warm-up
and exercise portions of the animal's training session.

and competitions. Join 4-H, U.S. Pony Club, or Future Farmers of America
(FFA). If your ambition is to train wildlife, volunteer at an aquarium, zoological park, or marine research facility. The National Zoo in Washington DC
has summer volunteer programs for teens. Check with your local zoo to see if
it offers one, too (most do!). Experts suggest trying to work with many different types of animals in various settings. A wide range of experiences will help
you decide what kind of animals you want to train and the techniques you do
and *don't* want to use.

Choosing Your Track

As we've mentioned, although animal trainers in the United States are not legally bound to get a particular type of education, many employers do have hiring requirements. Zoos and aquariums typically want trainers to have at least a four-year college degree, called a bachelor's degree. Most marine mammal facilities also prefer trainers have a bachelor's degree, and some require it. A college degree is not usually necessary for dog and horse trainers. However, experts say there are a number of reasons why everyone who seeks to train animals can benefit from a college education.

First, earning a bachelor's degree provides a solid background in animal behavior, human psychology, and the sciences. Second, it gives students more career options for earning a living. The U.S. Department of Labor reports the average annual salary for an animal trainer is about $30,000 a year, which is $15,000 less than what the average full-time American worker earns. Because the average pay for animal trainers is on the low side, a trainer may need to have a "day job" or second job to help make ends meet. College students are advised to study animal sciences along with another area that they enjoy that can provide a more substantial income. Finally, a college education can help open doors in this competitive industry. A degree may give someone an edge when applying for a job, lend credibility for a self-employed trainer working to attract clients, or pave the way to teaching at the college level.

The rest of this chapter is divided into the major areas of the field: dog trainer, horse trainer, marine mammal trainer, or zookeeper (training animals in a zoo falls under the job description of zookeeper). Find your dream job, then read about the educational options and recommendations for that career.

This golden retriever is undergoing the rigors of rescue-dog training. After training, he will be able to accomplish the work of 20 to 30 human searchers.

Dog Trainer

The education involved in becoming a professional dog trainer usually includes a combination of schooling, seminars, conferences, and hands-on work under the supervision of a mentor trainer.

Aspiring dog trainers may choose to enroll in a dog-training program offered by an independent school. The Association of Pet Dog Trainers (APDT) does not endorse any particular school, but advises that a good training program should consist of a balance of lectures, reading assignments, and hands-on training. "People think that they can go to an online school for a few weeks and go out and become a professional trainer and see clients, and that's just not enough education or preparation," explains Mychelle Blake, executive director of the APDT. "We often see people starting out as trainers fail in their businesses within the first few years because they did not do enough research and preparation." Blake says a school's curriculum should cover the history of dog training, the fundamentals of how animals learn, and dog behavior (including body language and breed characteristics). It should also teach the business aspects of the profession, such as creating a business plan, designing group classes, and marketing your services. For more tips and resources, visit APDT online.

Dog trainers may also choose to earn a college degree. Some students complete a two-year associate's program at a community college, though many elect to further their studies and earn their bachelor's degree. As we've explained, a bachelor's degree offers numerous benefits. Studying for this degree requires selecting a major, or a specific area of study. Recommended majors for a career in animal training include animal sciences, animal behavior, animal management, psychology, biology, or zoology. During college, students are advised to volunteer or do an **internship** at a rescue organization, veterinary clinic, or animal shelter. Katenna Jones, APDT's education programs coordinator, believes every dog trainer should hone their skills at an animal shelter. "There are millions of dogs out there that need training, and the training will save their lives," she says. "It's a boot camp for trainers. If you can successfully train a variety of shelter dogs and do it with kindness and love, and teach their future humans how to carry on, you are a good trainer."

After the initial schooling is complete, new trainers often apprentice with a more experienced trainer. In time, they may choose to earn certification through a professional organization, such as the Association of Pet Dog Trainers, the International Association of Canine Professionals, or the National Association of Dog Obedience Instructors. To become certified, applicants must show evidence of significant teaching experience and pass a written test. They may also be asked to submit reference letters from clients and other trainers. Certifications are maintained through **continuing education** classes.

Horses are the first loves for many who later become trainers. This young equestrian gives her horse a break to graze.

Horse Trainer

Many horse trainers say they first got hooked on horses as children. They took riding lessons and joined 4-H or the U.S. Pony Club. Some went on to compete in equestrian shows or sporting events. During and following high school, they apprenticed for several years with a professional trainer. Many also earned a degree, perhaps, from a vocational program at an independent equine school or a college or university.

Professionals advise aspiring horse trainers to earn a two-year associate's degree or four-year bachelor's degree in equine science, equine management, or animal science. When choosing a college or university, look for a curriculum that covers horsemanship, horse handling and training, genetics, reproduction, nutrition, and stable management. Hands-on experience should be part of the class work. Horse trainers must be advanced-level riders, so you should continually be improving your riding skills. The school's horse barn should be located within a few miles of campus. It should have an arena, trails, and plenty of horses so you can ride daily. A few colleges, such as the University of New Hampshire and West Texas A&M University, allow students to bring their own horses to campus. Ask about a student-run equestrian club or, if you are interested in competition, an equestrian team.

It's a Jungle in Here

Interested in training wildlife? Moorpark College, a community college in Southern California, offers an associate's degree in exotic animal training and management. The two-year program covers animal care and handling, behavior, training, and public education. As part of the curriculum, students are required to work at America's Teaching Zoo, a five-acre public zoo located on the Moorpark campus. Under the supervision of faculty and a professional staff, students work with nearly 200 different kinds of animals, from horses to lions to tortoises. They also conduct educational demonstrations for zoo visitors. Moorpark counselors advise graduates to continue their education and transfer to a university to earn a bachelor's degree.

"A good academic education is key, and it's not just about horses," says Sarah Hamilton, equine program director and dressage team coach at the University of New Hampshire. "In the equine industry, you must understand business—that's what makes this a vocation and not a hobby. Odds are good that at some point you'll be running a business for yourself or someone else." Hamilton also recommends students seek volunteer and internship opportunities, such as managing horses at a barn, assisting with a therapeutic riding program, or helping at horse shows.

Horse trainers do not need to be licensed, the exception being those who train racehorses. These trainers must be licensed by their state racing commission. Before receiving a license, a racing trainer must pass a test comprised of written and practical portions that demonstrates their knowledge of horses, equine health, racing equipment, terms, and regulations.

Following their initial education, horse trainers may choose to pursue certification in their specialty area from a professional organization, such as the Certified Horsemanship Association, the U.S. Hunter Jumper Association, or the U.S. Dressage Federation.

Marine Mammal Trainer or Zookeeper

Most zoos and aquariums, and many marine facilities, require their trainers to have a bachelor's degree. Marine mammal trainers and zookeepers, generally, major in one of the following areas: animal sciences, animal behavior, psychology, biology, marine biology, or zoology. Trainers who work at zoos, aquariums, marine parks, and research centers are also usually responsible for educating visitors. At SeaWorld parks, job applicants are even given a microphone test! To become comfortable speaking in public, students are advised to take courses in communication arts. Wildlife trainers need to be energetic, strong, and physically fit. Those who train marine mammals must also be proficient swimmers and hold Self Contained Underwater Breathing Appa-

Allie the dolphin often captivates audiences during marine mammal shows. Trainer Michaela Kluever guides Allie through tricks she performs at the Minnesota Zoo.

ratus (SCUBA) and Cardiopulmonary Resuscitation (CPR) certifications.

When selecting a college, students should look for one located near a zoological park, aquarium, marine facility, animal shelter, or wildlife sanctuary. It's not unusual for zookeepers and marine mammal trainers to be hired from the facility where they intern, volunteer, or work part-time. At Dolphin Research Center in Grassy Key, Florida, about one-quarter of the staff was hired from their volunteer/intern program. Log on to the Association of Zoos and Aquariums and the Alliance of Marine Mammal Parks and Aquariums websites for a list of facilities and links to their internship programs. For more detailed information about becoming a zookeeper, read *Zookeeper* in the Careers with Animals series.

Now that you've learned about the educational routes available for trainers, it's time to explore the major areas of the field and discover just what it takes to be a successful animal trainer.

THREE

Going to the Dogs

Almost 40 percent of American households have at least one dog, so it's no wonder that most dog trainers work with pets and the people who love them. A dog trainer may offer private training and/or group classes. He/she may also work as a behaviorist, helping to resolve problems such as aggression, shyness, destruction, fear, or anxiety. Some trainers work for obedience schools, pet stores, veterinarians, or shelters, but many are self-employed.

Salaries can vary widely for dog trainers, anywhere from $20,000 to more than $100,000 annually. "It can be a difficult way to make a living unless you invest time and money in learning some small-business skills as well, such as marketing, accounting, and public relations," says Mychelle Blake, executive director of the Association of Pet Dog Trainers. "Trainers who have a brick-and-mortar facility and offer a variety of services, such as boarding, grooming, and day care, tend to make more than others."

A Trainer's World

For a self-employed companion dog trainer, the day starts early. He/she is often at their desk by 7:00 a.m., working on case notes and handling business matters. The trainer reviews informational surveys submitted by new clients

(Opposite) These dogs are well behaved as
they take an exercise break in the park.

Part of dog obedience training is being taught to walk nicely while on a leash.

and notes for established ones. If the trainer is going to handle a behavioral issue, he/she will first have the client take their dog to a veterinarian for a physical exam. Some behavioral problems can stem from medical conditions, so it's important to rule them out before training begins.

By mid-morning, the car is packed with a trainer's tools of the trade: halters, leashes, **clickers**, treats, and toys. Some clients come to the trainer, although many trainers say they prefer to work with the dog in its environment. Each trainer has his/her own style and methods. Many trainers use **operant conditioning**, shaping behavior with consequences. They may use positive reinforcement (praise, petting, a treat, a toy), negative reinforcement (ignoring the behavior, a quick tug on the leash), or a combination of both. A trainer who wants to teach a dog how to leave something alone will first place a toy on the ground. With the dog on a leash, the trainer will walk the dog past the toy, speak the command "leave it," give a tug on the leash, and turn. At the precise moment the dog obeys, the trainer snaps the clicker (or says, "yes") and gives the dog a pat on the head, praise, or a treat. If the dog doesn't obey, the trainer starts over. Through repetition, the dog learns that the sound of the clicker (or a "yes") means he's done something right, and is about to get rewarded. In time, the behavior will become automatic and the dog won't expect a reward. "I love it when the animal gets what we're asking;

Heartbreak and Hope

Every trainer has been bitten, scratched, and kicked by an animal in training. It comes with the territory. Yet trainers say the biggest problems they face come not from animals, but people. Sometimes, an owner won't, or can't, do what's necessary to help correct a behavioral issue with their pet. Other times, the trainer is expected to solve a problem that's gone unchecked for far too long. This isn't always possible, and a trainer learns to say so. Also, it's not uncommon for trainers to work with shelter animals who have been mistreated. "It depresses and angers me, and I often feel helpless in the face of it," says trainer Shannon Finch. "But then I'll meet someone who has taken an animal in. That makes me feel a bit more hopeful. Working with animals has shown me the worst and best of humans."

Search and rescue dogs are trained in real-life field conditions. This rescue dog is being trained by a ski patroller to search avalanches.

when the light bulb comes on," says Shannon Finch, owner of AnimalKind training. "Sometimes I feel like a translator, helping humans understand what their animals are trying to express. Most people are doing the best that they can with their animals, and just need a little guidance, not judgment. I love it when someone says, 'Oh, now I understand why my dog, cat, or horse does that!'"

A private training session typically doesn't last more than an hour. The trainer may assign homework for an owner to do with the pet until the next

Join the Beagle Brigade

At the U.S. Department of Agriculture's National Detector Dog Training Center (NDDTC) in Georgia, a different breed of agricultural inspector is in training: beagles. At the center, training specialists teach beagles to either be alert, or sit down when they catch a whiff of mango, apple, orange, beef, and pork. These items are banned from entering the country because they may carry diseases and pests that could harm US agriculture. Each dog spends three months with a trainer before graduating to become part of the Beagle Brigade. The brigade patrols the nation's airports and border crossings, sniffing the luggage, boxes, and bags of travelers for illegal items (beagles are used because they are friendly and don't intimidate people). NDDTC training specialists are government employees with a yearly salary of $50,000 and up.

session. The number of clients a trainer sees in a day varies, depending on the training involved. "Behavior work is mentally and physically challenging, and I find I'm not at my best if I do more than a couple sessions a day," explains Finch.

By late afternoon, the trainer is on his/her way home to write up case notes and return phone calls and emails. Many clients have questions or concerns about their dog's progress and need guidance. A trainer may also have an evening obedience class or two to teach before finally calling it a day.

Argo, a trained bomb and patrol dog for the U.S. Navy, is being issued commands by his handler.

Lending a Paw

Some dog trainers specialize in teaching dogs to perform public service duties. Dogs have 250 million scent receptors in their noses compared to our 5 million, making them far more sensitive to odors than humans. With their eagerness to please and keen sense of smell, dogs can be taught numerous tasks. Their skills range from sniffing out drugs hidden in luggage to pinpointing the source of an arson fire to finding victims trapped beneath the rubble of an earthquake. Dog trainers may instruct police dogs, military dogs, detector dogs, search and rescue dogs, or service dogs. Professionals may be self-employed or work for an employer, such as a dog training school, government agency, or the military. Training usually involves additional study through an accredited dog-training school or apprentice program for one to three years.

Nearly 3,000 dogs serve in the U.S. military at home and overseas. They protect soldiers, track down

Search and rescue dogs are trained to find the origin of a human scent and let the handler or trainer know where it is. Barnaby, a trained search dog, is on the Red River during a mission to locate a missing victim.

enemies, and uncover weapons, bombs, and drugs. Lackland Air Force Base in San Antonio, Texas, is home to the U.S. Department of Defense's Military Working Dog (MWD) program. There, trainers with the 341st Training Squadron evaluate puppies from the base breeding program and shelter dogs for military suitability. They teach basic obedience, as well as the specialized skills that a military dog must have, such as attack training, explosive and weapons detection, and search techniques. They even learn to parachute from airplanes. Service members must be in the security forces (military police) for about three years before applying to be a trainer in the MWD program.

In civilian life, service dogs provide assistance to those with physical or mental disabilities. A service dog may be trained to pull a wheelchair, turn on lights, or open cabinets. A dog can do hundreds of tasks for its owner—maybe even saving his/her life! When an epileptic person has a seizure, a trained seizure-response dog summons help, removes dangerous items from the area, and gives comfort to its owner. A diabetic service dog can be taught to alert its owner *before* the onset of the symptoms of low blood sugar: dizziness, confusion, and fatigue (the dog is trained to pick up this scent from a saliva swab taken from its owner when blood sugar gets low). A service dog trainer will work with a dog from six months to two years to prepare the animal for its prospective owner. Once initial instruction is complete, the trainer teaches the dog and its owner to work as a team. A trainer in this specialty must be precise and thorough, because someone's life could depend on it. "The most important thing one needs to become an effective service dog trainer is empathy toward others—the desire to help and the ability to inspire," says Mary McNeight, founder of Service Dog Academy. To enter this area of the field, an experienced dog trainer will apprentice with an organization that trains service dogs for two to three years.

Professionals say it takes a dedicated person to be a dog trainer. You'll work long hours for low pay. You'll get covered in slobber and fur. You'll deal with pet owners who will expect you to work miracles. But the sacrifices, they say, are worth it. There is nothing better, says dog trainer Katenna Jones, than "seeing a happy dog and a happy person together for life."

A K-9 member of the US-AID/Fairfax Urban Search & Rescue team searches for signs of someone alive at a collapsed building, working with other search teams from around the world at the Hotel Montana, Port-au-Prince, Haiti.

FOUR

In Step with Horses

Whether teaching a young horse to pick up her hoof or an older horse to overcome a fear of cows, a horse trainer's job is rarely dull. Horse trainers work with horses to allow the animals to be used for riding or work. They teach horses to respond to verbal commands and other cues, such as a gentle tug on the reins or a squeeze from a rider's legs. Horse trainers tend to specialize in a particular area, among them Western riding, English riding, showing or eventing, and racing. A trainer will either personally take care of the animals, or oversee those who do. From feeding to grooming to veterinary care, a trainer is involved in every aspect of a horse's well being.

The Department of Labor reveals the average annual salary for a horse trainer is about $30,000, but because trainers are generally self-employed, the pay can vary widely. Many factors can come into play, such as the number of horses the trainer works with on a regular basis, level of experience, working arrangements, and additional income sources. Many trainers rent space, paying a stable owner a fee to train horses at their facility. Some trainers own their own barns and **board** the horses they train. Other potential income sources for a trainer include participating in horse shows, evaluating horses

(Opposite) It takes patience to prepare a horse for a ride. The horse has to be well groomed before it is ready to be mounted.

And They're Off!

A small segment of horse trainers specialize in training horses for the racing industry. A racehorse trainer is responsible for a horse's daily care, developing and overseeing a workout schedule, and coaching the jockey on how to get the best performance from the animal on the track. It's a pressure-packed job. In this high-stakes sport, trainers are expected to produce horses that win. In addition to their standard fees, racehorse trainers also receive a percentage of their horses' winnings. Salaries may vary from a few thousand dollars a year to $1 million or more for top trainers. That said, this field is extremely competitive. Only a lucky few trainers will ever know what it feels like to have a horse run in the Kentucky Derby.

A rider of the *Spanische Hofreitschule Wien* (Spanish Riding School of Vienna) performs a white Lipizzaner stallion in Vienna.

for buyers, selling horses for clients, and giving riding lessons. Trainers may also buy horses to train and sell for profit.

Horses are expensive animals to keep and train, so the client base for this field is limited. Add to that the popularity of the profession—there are a lot of horse trainers out there—and it can be a tough way to earn a living. "Every trainer and instructor in my area (the southern tier of New York) that has a stable [also] has a significant backup income, either a second job, or a significant other, that helps sustain a lifestyle," reveals Gale Wolfe, a horse trainer and riding instructor. Gail has owned horses since childhood, but decided to get her college degree in environmental engineering so she could make a living. Once her career was established, she was able to finance her dream: owning her own stable. She says students should get a good education in equine science as well as a backup occupation. "After your schooling, hitch your wagon to an already successful stable, and then do everything that you can to support the owner of that stable, and learn everything that you can," advises Gale. "Become an asset to that stable so that clients will come to the stable, not just for the stable, but for you, too. You'll have less stress and will make more money if you are a trainer and instructor in a successful stable than if you actually own the facility yourself."

Saddle Up!

With every horse in training, there are goals to be met. A trainer's job is to develop and execute a plan to reach them. A trainer may prepare a horse for competition or provide regular exercise for a horse whose owner can't get to the stable every day. One might be asked to "start" a horse, meaning teach a horse that has never been ridden to accept a halter, saddle, and other riding equipment, and then a rider. Or a trainer may work with a "finished" horse, sharpening skills the animal already knows and showing him new ones. Trainers teach horses how to accept being tied to a post, to stand still, and other good manners. They may also help resolve behavioral problems, such as biting, bucking, or spooking.

Training a horse means thinking like one. Horses are herd animals, so it's natural for them to seek a leader. They are also prey animals and are easily frightened. A trainer takes on the role of leader, not to instill fear in the animal but to build a relationship of mutual trust and respect. "Horses need to have a say in what they are asked to do," explains Gincy Bucklin, who has been training and riding horses for more than 60 years. "If you build a good relationship with a horse, which is exactly the same kind of a relationship you want to have with people that you work with closely, the horse will do his best to work with you." A new behavior is taught by breaking it down into a series of small steps, using repetition and praise to help the horse learn. "You never see any conflict, because the trainer never asks the horse for anything that he isn't ready to do," says Bucklin. "Everybody always looks comfortable, competent, and confident."

A Day in the Life

It might seem glamorous to ride horses all day, but being a trainer is hard work. Each morning, trainer Melissa "Mel" Harms-Grossman is at the barn by 8:30 a.m. to meet with the barn crew and owner to discuss sick and injured horses, lessons and training needs, and new clients. She'll then contact existing clients, respond to e-mails, and return telephone calls. By 9:00 a.m., she is training her first of eight horses, or more. Mel works with each horse for at least one hour. In the summer, to keep things moving, a youth helper saddles the next horse in line, makes the exchange, and unsaddles the horse Mel has just ridden. Two nights per week, from 4:00 to 9:00 p.m., Mel teaches group and private riding lessons. Then it's an hour drive home to get some sleep and be ready for another busy day of training!

A Trainer's Gift

When an old friend asked horse trainer Melissa "Mel" Harms-Grossman about starting a young horse for him that he'd just purchased, she readily agreed. Mel's friend was paralyzed from the mid-chest down, so he couldn't cue a horse with his legs the way riders usually do. Mel figured he'd bought a quiet horse—one that she could teach to accept his modified saddle with a seatbelt.

The horse Mel met wasn't anything like the one she expected. Cutter, a four-year-old quarter horse, was not quiet. He had bucked and scared another horseman, who had tried to start him under saddle. Cutter also had some issues with spooking, especially at loud noises. This made him less than ideal for a paralyzed rider. Still, Melissa forged ahead with her promise to train him. She started with ground matters, teaching Cutter to be patient when he was tied. In the round pen, they worked on such things as turning, speeding up, slowing down, and stopping. She slowly introduced new items near and on his body, such as a saddle, until he accepted them. During their sessions, Cutter tried some of his old tricks. "We worked through the bucking," says Mel, "because I refused to come off!" Mel taught Cutter to walk over plastic tarps, around cones, over logs, and through water. To get him to tolerate noise without spooking, she repeatedly played a desensitizing CD with various sounds—kids crying, dogs barking, and traffic noises. After a few months of training, Cutter was making good progress. "He was moving beautifully, a smooth horse, and perfect for someone in need of a steady ride," she recalls.

The real test, however, came when Mel took Cutter to compete in a horse show. She entered him in the walk-jog-lope class (a lope is a three-beat run). They were doing fine with the walk and jog, and it looked as if Cutter might earn a ribbon! Then it was time to pick up speed and lope.

(Opposite) Historically, horses were groomed for warfare, farm work, sports, and transport. Today they are trained to perform more personal tasks that include therapeutic horseback riding for people with disabilities.

Cutter took off, exactly as Mel cued him, when, suddenly, a piece of the rein broke. When equipment breaks, a rider and horse are disqualified unless they can finish the competition without it. Mel knew Cutter probably couldn't do that. They weren't far enough along in his training. "So I took a deep breath, sat down, said, "whoa," and hoped for the best," says Mel. And she got it. The horse stopped dead in his tracks. "Cutter could have taken major advantage of that situation—and the old Cutter would have," she explains. "The new Cutter, however, did his job and did it with tolerance, exactly what a paralyzed person needed in a horse. It was a great reward for a trainer and a guy who had a hunch about a horse."

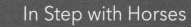

A young horse kicks out explosively while on the lunge line, Thomas Farm, Medina, Minnesota.

FIVE

Making a Splash

Loriel Keaton remembers the day when eleven veterans from the Wounded Warrior Project arrived at Florida's Dolphin Research Center, where she serves as director of animal care and training. The Wounded Warrior Project aids some of the U.S. military's most severely injured service men and women in their recovery and transition back to civilian life. "These men had all experienced the dark side of war," recalls Keaton. "When I first met them, they said very little. They rarely smiled." But after three days of swimming and communicating with the center's colony of bottlenose dolphins, something happened. "On their final morning the veterans got to play on surfboards and inflatable boats in our front lagoon," she says. "As the dolphins played with them in the water, not only did they smile, but they laughed. Our dolphins brought them joy again. It was unforgettable."

Keaton knows the profound ways animals can affect people. By age five, she already knew she wanted a career working with dolphins. "It's a passion that never wavered as I grew up," she explains. Keaton earned a bachelor of science in marine biology and gained experience training service dogs and working in veterinary clinics.

Now, Keaton oversees a staff of sixteen trainers at the center, caring for the twenty-two dolphins and three sea lions that live in the 90,000

(Opposite) Dolphin trainer Loro Parque balances on one bottlenose dolphin (underwater) as he feeds another.

Saviors of the Sea

U.S. college students seeking a career training marine mammals can apply for the U.S. Navy Marine Mammal Program (NMMP) internship. Based in San Diego, California, the NMMP trains bottlenose dolphins and California sea lions to detect and mark sea mines that could explode if ships came in contact with them. The Navy selects students from across the country to participate in the four-month internship. Interns work 40 hours per week, helping with research projects, feeding, sanitation, and open ocean training. To learn more about the internship, visit the NMMP website.

square-foot (8,360 square meters) seawater cove. Each day, Keaton and her team conduct training sessions to keep the marine mammals healthy and active. Often, the sessions include participation from visitors, as it did with the veterans. These interactive programs are a favorite of Keaton's. "It gives me the opportunity to share our wonderful marine mammal family with others and teach them about conservation," she explains. "Often for the folks that visit our facility, meeting a dolphin is a lifelong dream. It is a privilege to share those moments with them."

If you are planning for a career as an animal trainer, it is important to gain as much hands-on experience with animals as possible. High school student Justin Risica takes a lesson on beluga whales from trainer Justin Richard at the Mystic Aquarium in Mystic, Connecticut.

Sink or Swim!

Marine animal trainers work with dolphins, porpoises, whales, seals, sea otters, sea lions, and other sea mammals. They are employed by aquariums, marine parks, research centers, and rescue and rehabilitation facilities around the globe. However, because of the overwhelming popularity of this career, the competition for jobs is stiff. Several hundred people apply for the handful of trainer jobs available each year at SeaWorld Parks in California, Texas, and Florida. At smaller facilities, such as Dolphin Research Center, a new trainer is hired about

Feed Me!

Most marine mammal facilities feed their animals three meals a day. At some places, workers sort, weigh, and prepare the fish, but in others, one or more of these chores falls to the trainers. Each day, a sea lion eats 5 to 8 percent of its body weight, or between 15 and 35 pounds (7–16 kg) of food. Dolphins eat about 4 to 6 percent of their body weight, or about 16 to 25 pounds (7.3–11 kg) of fish. Trainers typically handle all of the feedings and must be able to carry a bucket filled with up to 50 pounds of fish and ice.

every two years. Applicants with a college degree in the sciences, experience with animals, SCUBA and CPR certifications, a marine mammal internship, and good communication skills have the edge.

It takes many hours of volunteering, interning, and part-time work to finally get the chance to become a trainer. Salaries in the field vary and are based on the size, location, and type of facility (profit vs. nonprofit). Entry-level positions pay about $18,000 per year. Trainers with five or more years of experience can generally expect to make between $25,000 and $50,000 per year.

Water World

Humans train marine mammals to learn about the behavior, abilities, and habits of these fascinating creatures. Also, a captive marine mammal's health and well-being depend on proper training. At work, a trainer must be positive, patient, and enthusiastic. Dolphins are intelligent creatures and can quickly sense changes in their trainer's mood or energy level. Trainers communicate with marine mammals verbally, using hand signals, and with whistles. It's common to use operant conditioning and a whistle to train behaviors (a clicker is hard for animals in the water to hear). The moment the requested behavior is demonstrated, the whistle is blown and the animal is rewarded with a fish or praise. To develop relationships, a trainer may conduct several sessions a day, each with a different animal. Sometimes, several trainers will work with a group of animals.

Keeping marine animals healthy requires regular veterinary checkups. To make these easier to do, a trainer teaches an animal specific behaviors, such as holding still, turning over, opening its mouth, and lifting its fins or tail. These cooperative behaviors allow a veterinarian to examine the teeth and body, take a blood or blowhole sample, give vitamins or medication, and perform procedures without causing the animals stress.

In the ocean, dolphins expend a great deal of energy swimming and hunting for food. In an environment where space is limited and food is provided, it's important for them to get plenty of exercise. It's a trainer's job to lead the animals through various swimming, jumping, and diving activities. Mental stimulation is vital, too. Dolphins can become easily bored. Trainers regularly devise new games, puzzles, and other sports to challenge these clever creatures, and always vary the daily routine.

About half of a marine mammal trainer's day involves working with animals. The other half is spent doing chores. These includes feeding the animals, scrubbing fish coolers, cleaning the habitat, disinfecting food preparation areas, testing for water quality, and observing and recording animal behavior. Marine mammal trainers typically work an eight- to ten-hour day, but are on-call twenty-four hours a day. They must be able to work nights, weekends, and holidays, too. After all, animals need round-the-clock care!

Now that you have a good idea of what is involved in training marine mammals, do you still envision yourself in this career? If so, good. More than anything, someone who plans to enter this popular field needs perseverance. "Never give up," advises trainer Loriel Keaton. "Passion, determination, and dedication will get you there. Never let anyone tell you that you can't do it."

(Opposite) This student makes a splash as she befriends a bottlenose dolphin.

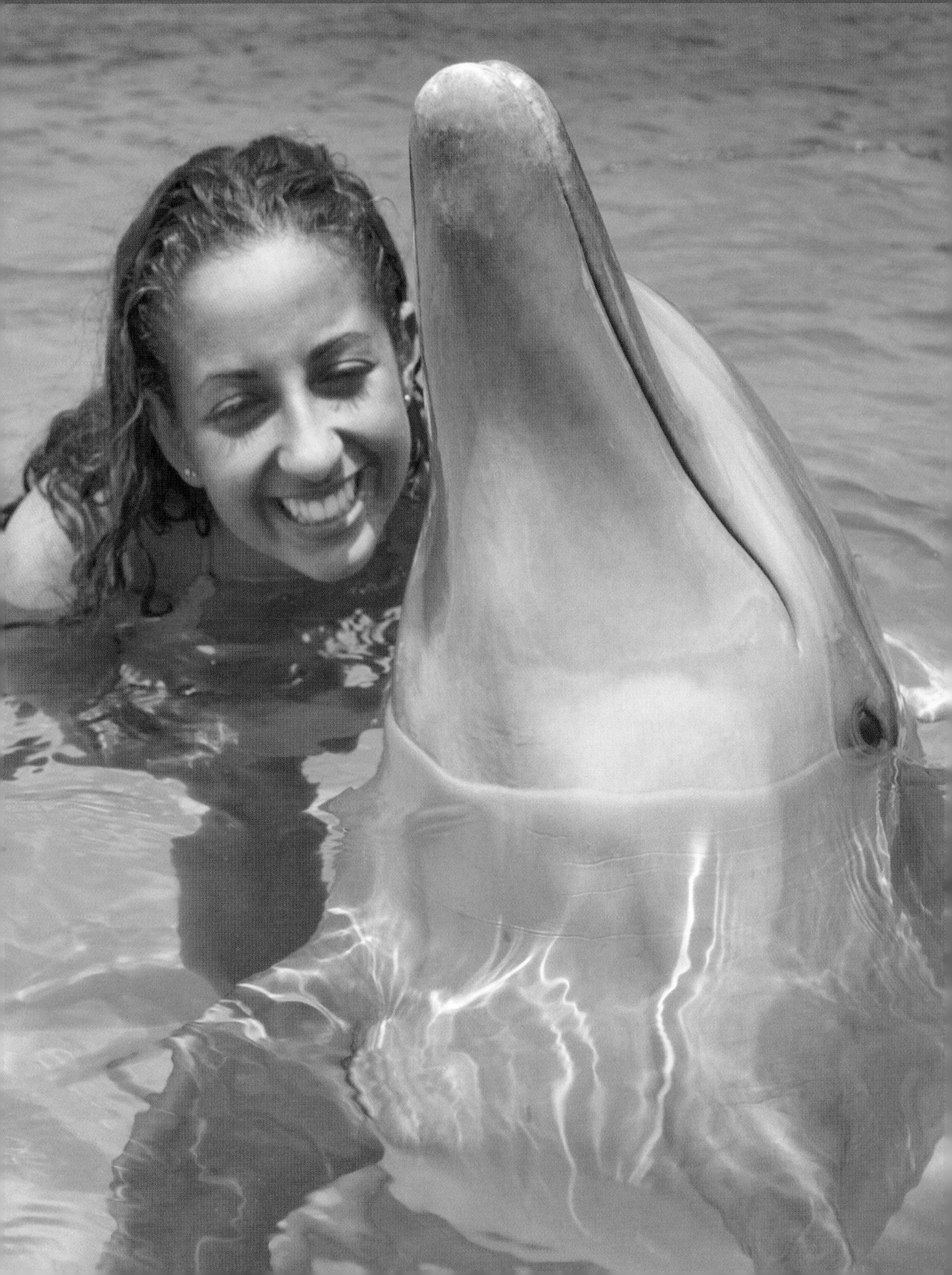

SIX

What Does the Future Hold?

For those planning to enter the animal training profession, the employment forecast is a bit gloomy. The U.S. Bureau of Labor Statistics reports overall employment of animal trainers is expected to increase no more than 9 percent between now and 2020, adding less than 4,200 jobs to the economy. This is slower than the average rate for all other occupations. Still, the outlook is brighter for some areas of the field than others.

It's projected that the biggest demand within the industry will be for dog trainers. The American Pet Products Association's National Pet Owners Survey reveals Americans own 78 million dogs, and the number is steadily climbing. Statistics show that in 2012, Americans spent more than $50 billion on their pets, almost double what they spent a decade ago. As Americans adopt more dogs, and lavish more on them, the need for qualified companion dog trainers will rise, too. Larger pet stores, private obedience schools, and animal shelters will be among the employers hiring.

One emerging area is service dog trainers, who teach clients to train their own service dogs. Currently, someone who wants a service dog may have to pay several hundred to several thousand dollars, and be placed on a waiting list for up to five years. Clients who are able and willing to do the bulk of the

(Opposite) A guide dog is trained to maintain a direct route and ignore distractions such as smells, other animals, and people. Walking to the left and just ahead of the handler, they stop at all curbs until told to proceed.

On the Trail

Dog trainers are on the front lines of wildlife research, thanks to programs such as Conservation Canines (CK9). Developed by the University of Washington's Center for Biology, CK9 teaches shelter dogs to find animal scat, or droppings. Scientists then collect and analyze the scat to learn about an animal's diet and health. The CK9 training facility is located on 4,300 acres at the base of Mount Rainier in Washington State, an area perfect for wilderness training. It takes a couple of months for a trainer to teach a shelter dog to sniff out the scat of one or more species. Once instruction is complete, the trainer-dog team goes on location to track scat, perhaps to Asia, Africa, or even to the ocean (to find orca scat!). CK9 trainers typically have a bachelor's degree in science, and several years of experience in wildlife conservation.

training themselves can considerably cut both the cost and wait-time for a service animal.

The future also appears promising for those interested in training dogs for law enforcement, homeland security, and the military. Prior to the September 11, 2001, terrorist attacks, the 341st Training Squadron at Lackland Air Force Base trained about 200 dogs each year for the U.S. Military Working Dog Program. Today, more than 800 dogs are in training at any one time, as instructors scramble to keep up with demand for soldier dogs at home and overseas. At the U.S. Department of Agriculture's National Detector Dog Training Center (NDDTC) in Georgia, the staff has recently doubled in size. Trainers at the NDDTC teach dogs to sniff out contraband meat and fruit products at the nation's ports, borders, and postal facilities. The agency is also now training detector dogs for other nations, such as Mexico, Japan, and South Africa.

Unfortunately, the job outlook for other animal training specialties is not as favorable. The Department of Labor reports the demand for horse trainers, marine mammal trainers, and zookeepers will grow at a far slower pace than dog trainers. Government findings indicate the limited number of job openings, combined with the popularity of these careers, will lead to far more applicants than available positions.

Following Your Dream

The road to becoming an animal trainer may seem daunting. But many people succeed in this field, and so can you. Experts say keeping a few things in mind will help you achieve your goal. First, while you have the time and don't have to worry about supporting yourself financially, take every opportunity you can to gain real-world experience with animals. Train your cat or dog. Volunteer at a stable. Go to marine mammal trainer

Sea turtles do not typically grace New England shores unless they are seriously debilitated. This 40-pound (18 kg) loggerhead turtle gets a lift from volunteer Deirdre Witkowski back to its pool at New England Aquarium's Animal Care Center in Quincy, Massachusetts.

summer camp. Read books, watch DVDs, and absorb as much knowledge as you can.

Next, make a plan to get a good education in animal sciences as well as in an area you like that will allow you to make a living. Start training animals in your spare time, then gradually work your way into full-time work.

Finally, stay focused and determined. "There's no way to sugarcoat it—it's a tough business and you have to be really, really dedicated and want it," says Sarah Hamilton, equine program director at the University of New Hampshire. "The students who are successful are hungry for knowledge, excited to be working in the field, and willing to go the extra mile to get there. Students also have to be willing to get up early, work long hours, get dirty, and do physical labor. It isn't for everyone. You have to be tough and hardy, and not easily discouraged. You have to be willing to spend your life learning and grow your career step by step."

With experience, education, and a solid plan you can achieve your dream. You can have a career bringing humans and animals together to enrich their lives, and yours.

Going Solo!

The U.S. Department of Labor reports nearly one-third of all animal trainers are self-employed. It may seem scary to be responsible for every aspect of your income, from accounting to advertising, but it can be lucrative if you do it wisely. Start slowly. Work part-time at first. Seek out a mentor, someone who is a successful trainer that you can go to when you have questions or need guidance. Market yourself well. Create a website, along with marketing materials to distribute. Ask clients who are satisfied with your work for testimonials you can use to attract new clients. Always be professional, punctual, and reliable. As your reputation grows, so will your business.

Glossary

apprenticed	to have worked under the supervision of a more experienced professional for the purpose of learning a trade
board	to provide with food, shelter, and other amenities for a fee
canine	relating to dogs
clickers	small, metal, handheld devices that make clicking noises when pressed
continuing education	classes professionals take following their initial training to advance their knowledge and skills

dog agility   a competitive sport where dogs complete an obstacle course for time and accuracy

equine   relating to horses

internship   paid or unpaid programs in a professional workplace, in which students receive college credit in return for their work

operant conditioning   a method of animal training that relies on providing instant feedback to the animal in order to produce a desired behavior

service dog   a specially trained dog that assists someone who has a physical or mental disability

Find Out More

Books

Field, Shelly. *Career Opportunities: Working with Animals*. New York: Checkmark Books, 2012.

Otfinoski, Steven. *Zookeeper.* New York: Cavendish Square, 2014.

Thornton, Kim Campbell. *Careers with Dogs: The Comprehensive Guide to Finding Your Dream Job.* Irvine, CA: BowTie Press, 2011.

Wilde, Nicole. *One-on-One: A Dog Trainer's Guide to Private Training.* Santa Clarita, CA: Phantom Publishing, 2011.

Websites

American Quarter Horse Association (AQHA)

www.aqha.com

Log on to learn more about youth activities, events, and competitions and how to prepare for them. You can also apply for an AQHA college scholarship.

Association of Pet Dog Trainers

www.apdt.com

This website offers career information, educational tips, and resources for students. Do a "trainer search" to find links to professional companion dog trainers in your area.

Alliance of Marine Mammal Parks and Aquariums (AMMPA)

www.ammpa.org

AMMPA lists member facilities that offer internship programs, along with links to their websites.

International Marine Mammal Trainers Association

www.imata.org

Read what the professionals have to say about preparing for a career as a marine mammal trainer. In the "careers" section you'll find a list of accredited facilities with animal training programs and their links.

Index

Page numbers in **boldface** are illustrations.

About the Author

Trudi Strain Trueit is the author of more than eighty fiction and nonfiction books for young readers. A former television journalist and weather forecaster, she enjoys writing about career exploration, health, weather, Earth science, and history. Look for her other titles in the Careers with Animals series: *Animal Physical Therapist*, *Veterinarian*, and *Wildlife Conservationist*. Trueit has a bachelor's degree in broadcast journalism and lives in Everett, Washington, with her husband and their two cats. Read more about Trueit and her books at www.truditrueit.com.